SUCCESSFUL COOKING

HEARTY STEWS

INDEX

Contents

Magnificent Stews

Simple, nutritious, versatile and delicious, stews, however humble their reputation, can be as exotic or adventurous as you please. Just observe some cooking basics and the rest is up to you: the possibilities are truly boundless.

There are few things so comforting as entering a kitchen where a pot is slowly simmering on the stove, filling the house with the wonderful aroma of flavoursome food gently bubbling to perfection.

And what could be easier? Select the meat of the day, brown it up, pop in some choice vegetables, sprinkle in some fresh herbs, simmer for a few hours, then serve up with some steamed vegetables, and maybe some crusty bread to mop up all those lovely juices. There you have it: a succulent, satisfying meal that will have your dinner companions begging for more.

For really mouthwatering results, always select the freshest ingredients available. Some more exotic ingredients need not be expensive, especially when in season, and any extra effort spent in shopping or preparation will be well rewarded with enhanced flavour. In any case, stews are so wonderfully economical, you can splash out on some wild condiments to keep in the pantry to surprise the jaded tastebuds of unsuspecting guests.

SMART CUTS

Inexpensive, tougher cuts of meat are perfect for stews as long, lazy simmering breaks down connective tissue and tenderises the meat.

Before cooking, trim the meat of fat and obvious sinew (these toughen on cooking and also cause the meat to shrink), then cut the meat into pieces of a similar size – but not too small, as meat shrinks during cooking. Remember too that once tender, overcooking can make meat tough and stringy.

THE STEW THICKENS

Once trimmed and cut, the meat is often coated in seasoned flour (plain flour tossed with salt and pepper) and quickly fried in oil, butter or a blend of both. This gives a crisp, golden coating and helps develop a lovely flavour, and it also thickens the stew from the very beginning so you won't need to thicken it at the end.

Don't coat the meat until you are ready to start cooking, as the moisture in the meat will absorb the flour and create a thick gluggy coating on the meat, affecting the whole dish. Also thoroughly shake off any excess flour from the meat before browning.

There are several ways of coating the meat with flour. One is to place the seasoned flour on a sheet of greaseproof paper and turn the meat in the flour. Another (much cleaner) method is to place the seasoned flour in a plastic bag, add the meat in batches, seal and give a good shake.

To coat meat, put in a bag with seasoned flour, seal and shake.

To make a beurre manié, mix butter into an equal quantity of flour to make a paste.

Brown the meat all over in a hot pan. Drain on paper towels.

Whisk small amounts of the paste into the sauce. Bring to the boil to thicken the sauce.

The meat is then quickly browned in hot oil. Browning seals the meat and also imparts a rich colour to the stew. Butter burns at a lower temperature than oil, but has more flavour, so using a blend of the two for browning is a neat compromise. Don't crowd the pan: the meat will stew in its juices and toughen.

Another way to thicken a stew, rather than flouring the meat first, is to brown the meat, remove it from the pan and stir flour into the pan juices until well browned. Adding liquid will then create a sauce which is poured over the meat.

Cornflour or a slurry (a thin paste of flour and water) can also be added to the stew as a thickener towards the end of cooking. Another option is to use a beurre manié – a paste made of equal quantities of butter and flour, whisked into the sauce once the vegetables and meat are removed. When using a slurry or a beurre manié, boil the sauce for a few minutes to cook the flour.

Probably the easiest way to thicken a stew is simply to remove the meat and simmer the liquid without a lid until it reduces down to a sauce.

LEAN CUISINE

Any fat on the surface of stews after cooking can be skimmed off with a metal spoon, or by dragging paper towels across the surface.

Refrigerating a stew overnight allows the fat to rise to the surface and solidify, making it very easy to remove before reheating.

STOCKS & SEASONINGS

A good quality stock can only make a stew taste better. Make your own, or use a prepared stock available in tetra packs.

Some speciality stores sell frozen home-made stock. Some pre-packaged stocks can be quite salty, so taste them before use: you may prefer to use half stock and half water. Stock cubes are a handy option and are sold in many flavours.

Instead of using salt and pepper for seasoning the flour, you could use paprika, celery salt, chilli or even stock powder – whatever suits the flavour of the dish you are cooking.

Extra seasoning can be added during cooking, but it is wise to wait until the dish is nearly done: flavours concentrate during cooking, and once added, they can't be removed.

IN THE POT

Heavy-based saucepans are perfect for stews as they spread heat evenly, and hold heat well. If using a casserole dish, ensure it has a tight-fitting lid to seal in flavours and moisture. Using a flame-proof dish – one that can go in the oven and cook on the stovetop as well – makes cooking a one-pot affair.

The stew is usually covered and simmered very slowly until tender; tiny bubbles should appear now and then on the surface.

STORAGE & FREEZING

Like many good things, most stews improve in flavour if cooked in advance and refrigerated, covered, for up to two days. They should be reheated gently over low heat, or microwaved on Medium-high (70%).

Some dishes thicken on standing or after refrigerating overnight. If this happens, the stew can be thinned down with a little stock or water while reheating – add a little at a time.

Some stews also make great fillings for pies. Choose a stew without bones, or cut the meat off the bones. (If the sauce is too thin for a gravy, thicken it with a thickener described before.) Spoon the filling into a pre-baked pastry case, top with a pastry lid and bake in a moderately hot oven (190°C/375°F/Gas 5) for 30–40 minutes, or until the pie is heated through and golden brown.

Most stews freeze for 3–6 months, except seafood and delicate Asian-style stews. Freeze in small portions or larger quantities to suit the number of people you generally cook for. Stews should be frozen as soon as they are cold.

To reheat, allow the frozen stew to thaw in the refrigerator overnight. If you are reheating it in a ceramic dish, place the dish in the oven while the oven is still cold, then bring the oven to moderate (180°C/350°F/Gas 4) to prevent the dish cracking.

If you are making extra quantities with the idea of freezing leftovers, remember that potatoes don't freeze well, and cream curdles on reheating. So if the stew has potatoes or dumplings, or is finished with cream before serving, leave out these ingredients, and instead add them when reheating the stew.

Line a bowl with a freezer bag, ladle in the cooled stew, seal the bag and freeze.

Moroccan Lamb Shanks

PREPARATION TIME: 25 minutes
TOTAL COOKING TIME: 3 hours 15 minutes
SERVES 4

Spicy Paste
30 g (1 oz) bunch coriander, roots intact
1 teaspoon ground turmeric
2 teaspoons ground cumin
1 teaspoon paprika
1 teaspoon ground coriander
½ teaspoon ground cinnamon
1 dried red chilli
2 cloves garlic, crushed
2 tablespoons honey
¼ cup (60 ml/2 fl oz) olive oil

light olive oil, for cooking
8 lamb shanks
3 onions, sliced into thick rings
sugar, for sprinkling
1 cup (250 ml/8 fl oz) white wine
2 cups (500 ml/16 fl oz) chicken stock
4 lime quarters, to garnish
coriander leaves, to garnish

1 In a food processor, blend the spicy paste ingredients (including coriander roots) to a smooth paste. Set aside.

2 Heat 3 tablespoons of oil in a large, heavy-based pan. Brown the shanks in batches over high heat and transfer to a large, ovenproof dish. Preheat the oven to moderate 180°C (350°F/Gas 4).

3 Heat a tablespoon of oil in the pan. Add the onion rings, sprinkle with sugar and sauté over medium heat for 10–15 minutes, or until golden.

4 Add the spicy paste and sauté for 2 minutes. Season well, add the wine and stock and simmer for 15 minutes.

5 Pour the wine sauce over the lamb shanks. Cover and bake for 1 hour, then turn the shanks over and bake for another 1½ hours, or until the meat is tender. Spoon any fat from the surface, transfer to plates and garnish with lime quarters and coriander leaves. Serve with couscous.

Blend the spicy paste ingredients in a food processor until smooth.

Heat the oil in a large pan. Brown the shanks over high heat.

Add the spicy paste to the fried onion and sauté for 2 minutes.

Hungarian Veal Goulash

PREPARATION TIME: 20 minutes
TOTAL COOKING TIME: 2 hours
SERVES 4

2 tablespoons olive oil
2 onions, chopped
500 g (1 lb) stewing veal, cubed
1 tablespoon Hungarian paprika
¼ teaspoon caraway seeds
425 g (14 oz) can tomatoes
2 cups (500 ml/16 fl oz) beef stock
1 large potato, diced
1 large carrot, thickly sliced
1 green capsicum, chopped
½ cup (125 g/4 oz) sour cream

1 Heat the oil in a large, heavy-based pan. Cook the onion for 10 minutes over medium heat, stirring from time to time, until soft and golden. Remove from the pan, increase the heat, then brown the veal in batches.

2 Return all the veal to the pan with the onion. Add the paprika, caraway seeds, chopped tomatoes and stock. Bring to the boil, reduce the heat, then cover and simmer for 1¼ hours.

3 Add the vegetables. Cook uncovered for 20 minutes, or until tender. Season to taste with salt and freshly cracked black pepper, and stir in the sour cream. Serve with rice or pasta.

Heat oil and fry onions over medium heat until soft.

Add paprika, caraway seeds, chopped tomatoes and stock.

Add vegetables and cook for 20 minutes, or until tender.

Beef and Globe Artichoke Stew

PREPARATION TIME: 30 minutes
TOTAL COOKING TIME: 2 hours 15 minutes
SERVES 4–6

2 tablespoons olive oil
1 kg (2 lb) stewing beef, cut into large
   cubes
2 red onions, sliced
4 cloves garlic, crushed
1 teaspoon cumin seeds
2 teaspoons ground cumin
1 teaspoon ground coriander
2 teaspoons sweet paprika
1 tablespoon plain flour
2 cups (500 ml/16 fl oz) beef stock
1 teaspoon grated lemon rind
1 tablespoon soft brown sugar
1 tablespoon tomato paste
¼ cup (60 ml/2 fl oz) lemon juice
4 fresh globe artichokes
3 tablespoons small black olives

1 Preheat the oven to moderate
180°C (350°F/Gas 4). Heat half oil
in a heavy-based pan. Brown meat in batches over
medium heat and transfer to a large casserole dish.

2 Add remaining oil to pan and cook onion for
5 minutes. Add garlic, cumin seeds, cumin,
coriander and paprika and cook for 1 minute.

3 Add flour, cook for 30 seconds and remove from
heat. Add stock, return to heat and stir until mixture
bubbles. Add to the meat with the rind, sugar and
tomato paste. Cover and bake for 1½ hours.

4 Meanwhile, add lemon juice to a bowl of water.
Cut the top third from each artichoke, trim stem
to 5 cm (2 inches) and cut away dark outer leaves.
Cut artichokes lengthways in half. Remove prickly
lavender-topped leaves in the centre and scoop
out the hairy choke. Drop into the lemon-water.

5 Drain artichokes and add to casserole, covering
them in the liquid. Cover and cook for 30 minutes,
or until tender. For a thicker gravy, cook uncovered
for 15 minutes more. Season and stir in the olives
to serve.

*Add garlic and spices to the fried
onion and cook for 1 minute.*

*Cut artichokes lengthways in half
and place them in lemon-water.*

*Drain artichokes and add to casse-
role, covering them with liquid.*

Pork and Mustard Stew

PREPARATION TIME: 15 minutes
TOTAL COOKING TIME: 1 hour 10 minutes
SERVES 4–6

2 tablespoons oil
1 kg (2 lb) pork neck, cut into
  3 cm (1¼ inch cubes)
20 g (¾ oz) butter
1 large onion, sliced
1 clove garlic, crushed
250 g (8 oz) button mushrooms, halved
1 tablespoon plain flour
⅓ cup (80 ml/2¾ fl oz) lemon juice
1 cup (250 ml/8 fl oz) chicken stock
2 tablespoons wholegrain mustard
2 teaspoons honey
½ teaspoon ground cumin

1 Preheat the oven to warm 170°C (325°F/Gas 3). Heat the oil in a large, heavy-based pan and brown the pork in batches over high heat. Transfer to a large casserole dish.

2 Add the butter to the pan and cook the onion and garlic until soft but not brown. Add the mushrooms and cook for 1 minute. Stir in the flour, then the remaining ingredients. Stirring, bring to the boil. Season to taste and spoon the mixture over the pork. Cover and bake for 45 minutes, or until tender.

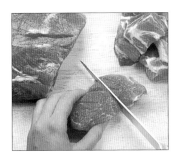

Using a sharp knife, cut the pork neck into large cubes.

Melt butter, add onion and garlic and cook until soft.

Stir flour into onion and garlic. Add remaining ingredients.

Navarin of Lamb

PREPARATION TIME: 25 minutes
TOTAL COOKING TIME: 1 hour 35 minutes
SERVES 4

8 lamb noisettes
plain flour, seasoned with salt and pepper
2 tablespoons oil
2 sticks celery, sliced diagonally into 2 cm
  (¾ inch) lengths
12 baby carrots, peeled
12 new potatoes, unpeeled
6 sprigs of thyme
¼ cup (15 g/½ oz) chopped parsley, and extra
  to garnish
2 onions, chopped
2 cloves garlic, crushed
⅓ cup (40 g/1¼ oz) plain flour
2½ cups (625 ml/21 fl oz) chicken stock
1 cup (250 ml/8 fl oz) good red wine
¼ cup (60 g/2 oz) tomato paste

1 Toss the lamb in the seasoned flour, shaking off the excess. Preheat the oven to moderate 180°C (350°F/Gas 4).

2 Heat the oil in a heavy-based pan. In batches, brown the lamb well on both sides over medium-high heat. Remove from the heat, drain well on paper towels, then transfer to a greased, 3 litre capacity ovenproof casserole dish. Top with the celery, carrots, potatoes, thyme and parsley.

3 Cook the onion and garlic in the same heavy-based pan, stirring over medium heat for about 5–10 minutes, or until the onion is soft.

4 Add the flour and stir for 1 minute, or until the onion is coated. Add the remaining ingredients and stir until the sauce boils and thickens. Pour the sauce over the lamb and vegetables. Bake, covered, for 1¼ hours, or until the lamb is tender. Carefully remove the string from the lamb; sprinkle with extra parsley to serve.

Add lightly floured lamb to the hot oil and brown well all over.

Add stock, wine and tomato paste to softened onion mixture.

Beef Bourguignon

PREPARATION TIME: 10 minutes
TOTAL COOKING TIME: 2 hours
SERVES 4–6

1 kg (2 lb) topside or round steak
plain flour, seasoned with salt and freshly
  ground pepper
3 rashers bacon, rind removed
oil, for cooking
12 pickling onions
1 cup (250 ml/ 8 fl oz) red wine
2 cups (500 ml/16 fl oz) beef stock
1 teaspoon dried thyme
200 g (6½ oz) button mushrooms
2 bay leaves

1 Trim the steak of fat and sinew and cut into 2 cm (¾ inch) cubes. Lightly toss in the seasoned flour to coat, shaking off the excess.

2 Cut the bacon into 2 cm (¾ inch) squares. Heat some oil in a large pan and quickly cook the bacon over medium heat. Remove the bacon from the pan, then add the meat and brown well in batches. Remove and set aside. Add the onions to the pan and cook until golden.

3 Return the bacon and meat to the pan with the remaining ingredients. Bring to the boil, reduce the heat and simmer, covered, for 1½ hours, or until the meat is very tender, stirring now and then. Remove the bay leaves to serve. Mashed potato and steamed green beans are a nice accompaniment.

Trim the meat of fat and sinew and cut into cubes.

Fry bacon in hot oil over medium heat until lightly browned.

Return bacon and meat to pan and add remaining ingredients.

Spiced Pork with Butter Beans

PREPARATION TIME: 25 minutes +
30 minutes soaking
TOTAL COOKING TIME: 1 hour 50 minutes
SERVES 4–6

200 g (6½ oz) dried butter or lima beans
1 large dried chilli
2 tablespoons oil
750 g (1½ lb) pork neck, cut into bite-sized
  pieces
2 teaspoons ground cumin
1 teaspoon ground coriander
2 onions, chopped
2 large potatoes, chopped
200 g (6½ oz) butternut pumpkin, peeled
  and cut into bite-sized pieces
1 large red apple, grated
3 cups (750 ml/24 fl oz) chicken stock
½ cup (125 ml/4 fl oz) cream

1 Soak the beans in boiling water for 30 minutes. In a separate bowl, soak the chilli in boiling water for 20 minutes. Drain the beans well and set aside. Chop the chilli and set aside.

2 Heat the oil in a large, heavy-based saucepan. Brown the meat in batches over medium-high heat. Remove from the pan with any juices and set aside.

3 Cook the spices, chopped chilli and onion in the pan for 5 minutes over medium heat, stirring often. Return the meat and any juices to the pan. Add the potato, pumpkin, apple and stock and season well with salt and freshly ground pepper. Cover and simmer over very low heat for 1 hour. Add the drained beans and simmer for 25 minutes, or until tender.

4 Stir through the cream and simmer, uncovered, for 10 minutes, or until the sauce is thick, stirring occasionally.

Using separate bowls, cover dried beans and chilli with boiling water.

Cook spices, chilli and onions over medium heat for 5 minutes.

Add drained beans to the casserole mixture. Simmer until tender.

Traditional Lamb Shanks

PREPARATION TIME: 30 minutes
TOTAL COOKING TIME: 2 hours 25 minutes
SERVES 4–6

8 lamb shanks
1 tablespoon olive oil
1 orange
1 large onion, sliced
4 cloves garlic
1 large carrot, cut into chunks
1 parsnip, cut into chunks
1 stick celery, cut into chunks
2 bay leaves
3 cups (750 ml/24 fl oz) chicken stock
2 cups (500 ml/16 fl oz) red wine
1 tablespoon redcurrant jelly
3 teaspoons cornflour
sprigs of thyme, to garnish

1 Preheat the oven to warm 160°C (315°F/Gas 2–3). Pat the shanks dry with paper towels. Heat the oil in a flameproof casserole or baking dish large enough to fit the shanks in a single layer, then brown the shanks over high heat for 3 minutes, turning frequently. Remove and set aside.

2 Peel three 5 cm (2 inch) strips of rind from the orange, avoiding the bitter white pith. Set aside.

3 Add the onion and garlic cloves to the dish and cook over medium heat for 2 minutes, stirring. Add the carrot, parsnip and celery and place the shanks snugly on top. Add the rind strips and bay leaves, then pour in the stock and red wine. Cover and bake for 2 hours, or until the meat is very tender and comes away from the bone.

4 Using tongs, carefully remove the shanks from the dish; cover with foil to keep warm. Remove the rind and bay leaves and strain the juices into a pan. Set the vegetables aside.

5 Add the redcurrant jelly to the dish and stir to dissolve. Boil rapidly for 20 minutes, or until the sauce is reduced to 1½ cups (375 ml/12 fl oz). Combine the cornflour with a little water and whisk into the sauce, stirring until thickened and glossy.

6 To serve, place the lamb shanks on serving plates, arrange the vegetables on top, drizzle with the sauce and garnish with thyme.

Heat the oil in a baking dish and brown the shanks over high heat.

Peel strips of rind from orange, avoiding the bitter white pith.

Hearty Pork and Red Lentils

PREPARATION TIME: 35 minutes
TOTAL COOKING TIME: 2 hours
SERVES 4–6

1 kg (2 lb) lean pork neck, sliced 2 cm
  (¾ inch) thick
plain flour, seasoned with salt and freshly
  ground pepper
50 g (1¾ oz) butter
1 tablespoon olive oil
1 large onion, finely chopped
3 cloves garlic, finely chopped
2 tablespoons chopped sage
1¼ cups (310 ml/10 fl oz) vegetable stock
1¼ cups (310 ml/10 fl oz) red wine
1 cup (250 g/8 oz) red lentils, rinsed
2 carrots, chopped
2 potatoes, chopped
3 sticks celery, chopped
1 bay leaf, torn in three
2 teaspoons finely grated lemon rind
2 tablespoons chopped parsley

1 Coat the pork in the flour, shaking off any excess. In a large, deep, heavy-based pan, heat the butter and oil over medium heat until foamy. Brown the pork well, in batches if necessary.

2 Return all the pork to the pan. Add the onion, garlic, sage, stock and wine; season well. Bring to the boil, turning the pork to coat in the liquid. Reduce the heat, cover and simmer for 1 hour, turning the pork during cooking. If the sauce becomes too thick, add about 1 cup (250 ml/8 fl oz) of water.

3 Add the lentils, carrots, potatoes, celery and bay leaf to the stew with 2 cups (500 ml/16 fl oz) of water, and plenty of salt and pepper. Bring to the boil, then reduce the heat to low. Simmer, covered, for 40 minutes.

4 Add the rind. Cook, uncovered, for 30 minutes, or until the sauce is thick and mash-like. If the pork is falling apart, remove and keep warm. To serve, pile the sauce onto the plates, rest some pork on top and sprinkle with parsley. Serve with mashed potato and steamed green beans.

Brown the pork well in the foamy butter and oil mixture.

When wine mix boils, turn pork over to coat in the cooking liquid.

Add lemon rind to the stew and cook, covered, for 30 minutes.

Spring Veal with Bacon and Zucchini

PREPARATION TIME: 20 minutes
TOTAL COOKING TIME: 1 hour 50 minutes
SERVES 4–6

3 medium leeks, thinly sliced
6 French shallots, chopped
2 cloves garlic, crushed
2 tablespoons chopped parsley
2 tablespoons chopped mint
200 g (6½ oz) small young zucchini, thickly sliced
85 g (3 oz) butter
1 kg (2 lb) thin leg veal slices
4 rashers lean bacon
⅓ cup (80 ml/2½ fl oz) cream
4 baby zucchini, with flowers

1 Combine the leeks, shallots, garlic, parsley, mint and sliced zucchini. Spread a thin layer in a deep, oiled ovenproof dish; season well. Preheat the oven to warm 170°C (325°F/Gas 3).

2 Gently melt the butter in a pan until golden brown with a nutty aroma. Remove from the heat.

3 Cut the veal into 9 cm (3½ inch) pieces, brush with the browned butter and season well. Overlap a veal layer over the vegetables. Repeat the layers, finishing with a layer of vegetables.

4 Remove the rind from the bacon. Cut the bacon in half crossways and arrange over the vegetables. Cover and bake for 40 minutes. Pour the cream in around the edge, then bake, partially covered, for 40 minutes more.

5 Arrange the baby zucchini over the bacon rashers. Cover and bake for 15–20 minutes: the vegetables and veal will shrink in from the sides of the dish to form a mould. If the sauce is thin, simmer in a pan until thick. Cut the mould into portions and drizzle with the sauce to serve.

Brush veal with browned butter, then layer veal over vegetables.

Cut bacon in half crossways and arrange over top of vegetables.

Evenly pour the cream in around the edge of the dish.

Smoked Sausage and Kidney Bean Stew

PREPARATION TIME: 20 minutes
TOTAL COOKING TIME: 2 hours 30 minutes
SERVES 4–6

1 small red capsicum, halved
2 tablespoons olive oil
2–3 cloves garlic, crushed
1 large onion, thinly sliced
1 carrot, cut into cubes
420 g (14 oz) can kidney beans, rinsed and drained
2 cups (500 ml/16 fl oz) beef stock
1 tablespoon treacle
600 g (1¼ lb) piece speck or bacon
425 g (14 oz) can chopped tomatoes, juice reserved
2 tablespoons tomato paste
150 g (5 oz) smoked sausages

1 Grill the capsicum halves, skin-side-up, under a hot grill until the skin is black and blistered. Cool, then peel off the skin and dice the flesh.

2 Heat the oil in a large, heavy-based pan. Add the garlic, onion and carrot and cook, stirring, over low heat for 4–5 minutes without browning.

3 Add the beans, stock, treacle and freshly ground black pepper to taste. Slowly bring to the boil, then add the speck or bacon. Reduce the heat; cover and simmer for 1 hour. Stir through the undrained tomatoes and tomato paste and simmer for 30 minutes.

4 Place the sausages in a pan of cold water. Slowly bring to the boil, then drain and add to the stew. Simmer, uncovered, for 45 minutes, or until the sauce is thick and rich.

5 Remove the speck or bacon and sausages, using tongs. Slice them, removing any fat and skin, and return to the stew for serving. Serve hot.

Add the beans, stock, treacle and pepper to the onion mixture.

Simmer stew until rich and thick, then remove speck and sausages.

Remove skin and excess fat from speck. Slice sausages and speck.

Veal with Almonds and Mushrooms

PREPARATION TIME: 20 minutes
TOTAL COOKING TIME: 1 hour 50 minutes
SERVES 4–6

75 g (2½ oz) blanched almonds
olive oil, for cooking
2 onions, chopped
1 kg (2 lb) diced veal
plain flour, seasoned with salt and freshly
    ground pepper
½ cup (125 ml/4 fl oz) red wine
500 g (1 lb) very ripe tomatoes, chopped
2 tablespoons chopped oregano
50 g (1¾ oz) butter
400 g (13 oz) mushrooms (such as tiny
    buttons, shiitake or porcini)

1 Preheat oven to 150°C (300°F/Gas
2). Scatter the almonds on a baking
tray and bake for 10 minutes, or
until golden. Cool and roughly chop.

2 Heat 2 tablespoons of oil in a deep,
heavy-based pan. Cook the onion
over low heat for 15 minutes, stirring often.
Remove and set aside, leaving as much oil as
possible in the pan.

3 Toss the veal in the flour, shaking off any excess.
Reheat the pan and brown the veal over medium
heat in batches, adding more oil if necessary.

4 Return all the veal to pan with any juices; add the
onion and wine. Bring to the boil and stir well.
Reduce heat to very low, cover with foil and a
tightly fitting lid, then simmer gently for 1 hour.

5 Stir well, then mix in the tomatoes and oregano.
Cover and simmer for another 20 minutes. Season
to taste.

6 Melt the butter until foamy in a frying pan over
medium heat. Cut any large mushrooms and cook
until just wilted, tossing well.

7 To serve, dish the stew onto serving plates, top
with the mushrooms, drizzle over any juices and
sprinkle with the chopped toasted almonds.

*Gently cook onion for 15 minutes.
Remove and set aside.*

*Return browned veal to pan with
juices. Add onions and red wine.*

*When butter is foaming, add the
mushrooms and cook until wilted.*

Rich Steak and Kidney Stew

PREPARATION TIME: 35 minutes
TOTAL COOKING TIME: 2 hours 30 minutes
SERVES 4–6

1 kg (2 lb) chuck steak, trimmed
8 lamb kidneys
¼ cup (60 ml/2 fl oz) oil
1 rasher bacon, rind removed, and cut into
   long, thin strips
40 g (1¼ oz) butter
1 large onion, chopped
300 g (10 oz) button mushrooms, halved
1 cup (250 ml/8 fl oz) Muscat
2–3 cloves garlic, crushed
¼ teaspoon ground allspice
½ teaspoon paprika
2 teaspoons coriander seeds, lightly crushed
1 tablespoon wholegrain mustard
1 cup (250 ml/8 fl oz) beef stock
2–3 tablespoons soft brown sugar
1–2 teaspoons thyme
1–2 teaspoons rosemary

1 Cut steak into 2–3 cm (1 inch) cubes. Cut kidneys in half, remove core and fat, then slice in half again.

2 Heat 1 teaspoon of the oil in a large, heavy-based pan. Add the bacon and cook over medium heat until just crisp. Remove and set aside.

3 Heat 2 tablespoons of the oil and 30 g (1 oz) of the butter in the pan. Brown the steak in batches and set aside.

4 Add onion to pan and cook for 3 minutes. Add the mushrooms and cook, stirring, for 3 minutes, until starting to brown. Stir in half the Muscat and simmer for 3–4 minutes. Remove and set aside.

5 Add the remaining oil and butter to the pan. Stir in the garlic, allspice, paprika and coriander and cook for 1 minute. Add the kidneys and cook until just starting to brown. Stir in the mustard and remaining Muscat and simmer for 2 minutes.

6 Stir in the bacon, steak, onion and mushrooms. Stir in the stock, bring to the boil, then reduce the heat, cover and simmer for 1 hour. Add the sugar.

7 Simmer, covered, for 40 minutes, then uncovered for 20 minutes, stirring in the herbs during the last 10 minutes.

Halve kidneys and remove the cores and fat. Slice in half again.

Add half the Muscat to onions and mushrooms and simmer.

Lamb Stew with Rosemary Dumplings

PREPARATION TIME: 25 minutes
TOTAL COOKING TIME: 2 hours
SERVES 4

8 lamb neck chops
plain flour, seasoned with salt and freshly
  ground pepper
2 tablespoons oil
2 rashers bacon, finely chopped
1 large onion, sliced
2 cups (500 ml/16 fl oz) beef stock
1 tablespoon chopped thyme
2 carrots, thickly sliced
2 potatoes, chopped

Rosemary dumplings
1 cup (125 g/4 oz) self-raising flour
20 g (¾ oz) butter, chopped
1 tablespoon chopped rosemary
⅓ cup (80 ml/2¾ fl oz) milk

1 Trim the lamb of fat and sinew and toss lightly in the flour, shaking off any excess. Heat the oil in a large, heavy-based pan, then brown the lamb in batches over medium-high heat. Remove and set aside.

2 Add the bacon to the pan and cook over medium heat for 2 minutes, or until brown. Add the onion and cook for about 5 minutes, or until soft.

3 Return the browned lamb to the pan. Add the stock, thyme and ½ cup (125 ml/4 fl oz) of water, then simmer, covered, over low heat for 30 minutes. Add the carrot and potato and simmer for 1 hour more.

4 To make the rosemary dumplings, sift flour into a bowl, then rub in the butter until mixture is fine and crumbly. Mix in rosemary. Add most of the milk and mix to a soft dough with a knife, adding more milk if needed. Turn out onto a lightly floured surface and gently knead until smooth. Divide dough into 12 portions and form into rough balls. Place dumplings on top of the stew, then cover and cook for 15 minutes. Serve immediately.

Lightly toss trimmed lamb in the flour, shaking off any excess.

Sift flour into a bowl. Rub in the butter until fine.

Divide dough into 12 portions, then form into rough balls.

33

Irish Stew

PREPARATION TIME: 20 minutes
TOTAL COOKING TIME: 1 hour 15 minutes
SERVES 4

8 lamb neck chops
4 thick rashers bacon, rind removed
30 g (1 oz) butter
1 kg (2 lb) potatoes, thickly sliced
3 carrots, sliced
3 onions, sliced into thick rounds
2 cups (500 ml/16 fl oz) beef or vegetable
  stock
sprigs of thyme or lemon thyme, to taste
chopped parsley, to garnish

1 Trim the chops of excess fat; cut the bacon into short strips. Melt the butter in a large heavy-based pan and brown the chops on both sides over high heat. Remove and set aside. Add the bacon to the pan and cook until crisp. Drain on paper towels.

2 Arrange half the potato, carrot and onion in a deep heavy-based pan. Season with cracked pepper, then add half the bacon. Layer the chops on top and cover with the remaining potato, carrot, onion and bacon. Add the stock and thyme.

3 Cover and bring to the boil, then reduce the heat and simmer for about 1 hour, or until the lamb is tender. Serve sprinkled with parsley.

Brown the chops on both sides in the hot butter over high heat.

Arrange half potato, carrot and onion in a heavy-based pan.

When the layers are complete, add the stock and thyme.

35

Beef Sausage and Mushroom Stew

PREPARATION TIME: 20 minutes +
30 minutes standing
COOKING TIME: 1 hour
Serves 4–6

15 g (½ oz) packet dried porcini mushrooms
12 thick beef sausages
300 g (10 oz) piece speck or bacon
2 teaspoons oil
2 onions, cut into eighths
8 cloves garlic
1 sprig of thyme
3 bay leaves
1½ cups (375 ml/12 fl oz) red wine
1 cup (250 ml/8 fl oz) beef stock
1 teaspoon Dijon mustard
1 bunch baby carrots
100 g (3½ oz) Swiss brown mushrooms,
 halved
100 g (3½ oz) button mushrooms, halved
1 tablespoon cornflour
chopped parsley, for serving

1 Soak the mushrooms for 30 minutes in enough boiling water to cover.

2 Brown the sausages well all over in a lightly oiled pan over medium heat. Drain on paper towels and place in a large, flameproof casserole dish.

3 Remove the rind from the speck or bacon; cut the meat into small strips. Heat the oil in a pan and add the speck, onions and garlic. Cook, stirring, until the onions are golden, then place in the casserole dish with the thyme, bay leaves, wine, stock and mustard. Cover, bring to the boil, then reduce the heat and simmer for 20 minutes.

4 Reserving 3 tablespoons of liquid, drain the mushrooms. Add the carrots and all mushrooms to the stew. Cover and simmer for 20 minutes. Mix the cornflour into the reserved liquid; stir into the stew until it boils and thickens. Sprinkle with parsley to serve.

Cover porcini mushrooms with boiling water and leave to soak.

Remove the rind from the speck and cut the meat into small strips.

Add carrots and all mushrooms to sausages. Simmer for 20 minutes.

Kidneys in Creamy Mustard Sauce

PREPARATION TIME: 15 minutes
TOTAL COOKING TIME: 25 minutes
SERVES 4

8 lamb kidneys
50 g (1¾ oz) butter
6 French shallots, finely sliced
1 cup (250 ml/8 fl oz) cream
2 teaspoons wholegrain mustard
2 teaspoons Dijon mustard
⅓ cup (20 g/¾ oz) chopped parsley

1 To prepare the kidneys, slice them in half lengthways. Using a pair of small sharp scissors, carefully snip out the core of each kidney and remove any membrane.

2 Melt half the butter in a small pan. Add the shallots and gently cook for 5 minutes, or until soft and golden. Add the cream and simmer for 10 minutes, or until reduced by one-quarter. Remove from the heat and stir in both mustards; mix well and set aside.

3 Melt the remaining butter in a frying pan over medium heat. When the butter foams, cook the kidney halves for 2 minutes on each side.

4 Pour the creamy mustard sauce over the kidneys and simmer, stirring, for 2 minutes. Stir in the chopped parsley and serve.

Cut kidneys in half lengthways and remove core and membrane.

Add the mustards to the cream and stir until well combined.

Pour the cream and mustard sauce over the kidneys.

Casserole of Autumn Vegetables

PREPARATION TIME: 25 minutes
TOTAL COOKING TIME: 30 minutes
SERVES 4–6

185 g (6 oz) frozen broad beans, thawed
150 g (5 oz) pickling onions
50 g (1¾ oz) butter
2 teaspoons olive oil
400 g (13 oz) small parsnips
150 g (5 oz) Jerusalem artichokes
2 tablespoons plain flour
2⅓ cups (600 ml/20 fl oz) chicken stock
300 ml (10 fl oz) cream
2 teaspoons grated lemon rind
1 teaspoon grated orange rind
400 g (13 oz) baby carrots, trimmed
500 g (1 lb) baby turnips, trimmed

1 Peel and discard the tough outer skin of the broad beans. Carefully peel the onions, leaving the flat root end attached, then cut a cross through the root end of each onion.

2 Heat the butter and oil in a large, heavy-based pan until foamy. Add the onions and cook for 7 minutes over low-medium heat, turning often to colour evenly.

3 While the onions are browning, peel the parsnips and artichokes and cut into bite-sized pieces. Add to the pan and toss well. Scatter with the flour, toss to coat and cook for 2 minutes.

4 Stir in the stock, cream and rinds. Bring to the boil, stirring, then reduce the heat and simmer for 7 minutes, or until the vegetables are half-cooked.

5 Add the carrots and turnips; toss well. Cover and cook for 4–5 minutes, or until the vegetables are just tender. Season well with salt and freshly ground pepper, stir in the broad beans to heat through, and serve.

Skin broad beans and cut a cross through root end of onions.

Peel the parsnips and artichokes and cut into bite-sized pieces.

Tomato and Potato Stew

PREPARATION TIME: 30 minutes
TOTAL COOKING TIME: 1 hour 15 minutes
SERVES 6

¼ cup (60 ml/2 fl oz) olive oil
2 red capsicums, chopped
2 green capsicums, chopped
3 onions, thinly sliced
4 cloves garlic, crushed
2 x 400 g (13 oz) cans chopped tomatoes
3–4 sprigs of thyme, and extra to garnish
2 bay leaves
2 teaspoons caster sugar
1.2 kg (2 lb 7 oz) potatoes, cut into chunks
1 cup (125 g/4 oz) black olives, pitted
small block of Parmesan, for shaving

1 Heat the oil in a large, heavy-based pan. When the oil is hot, cook the capsicum, onion and garlic over medium heat for 10 minutes, or until softened. Add the chopped tomatoes, ½ cup (125 ml/4 fl oz) water, thyme sprigs, bay leaves and sugar. Season to taste and leave to simmer gently for 15 minutes.

2 Add the potato chunks, cover and cook very gently for 50–60 minutes, or until tender. Stir in the olives.

3 Using a vegetable peeler, carefully shave thin slivers from the Parmesan block, arrange over the stew and garnish with a sprig of thyme.

When oil in pan is hot, fry onion, capsicum and garlic until soft.

Add the potato chunks to the tomato sauce mixture.

Using a vegetable peeler, shave slivers from the Parmesan block.

Vegetable Stew with Couscous

PREPARATION TIME: 30 minutes
TOTAL COOKING TIME: 45 minutes
SERVES 4

2 tablespoons olive oil
1 onion, sliced
2 teaspoons yellow mustard seeds
2 teaspoons ground cumin
1 teaspoon paprika
1 clove garlic, crushed
2 teaspoons grated fresh ginger
2 sticks celery, chopped
2 carrots, peeled and chopped
2 small parsnips, peeled and cubed
300 g (10 oz) pumpkin, diced
2 zucchini, halved and thickly sliced
1½ cups (375 ml/12 fl oz) vegetable stock
1 cup (185 g/6 oz) instant couscous
30 g (1 oz) butter, diced
harissa, to taste

1 Heat the oil in a large, heavy-based pan. Add the onion and cook over medium heat for 10 minutes, or until very soft and lightly golden, stirring occasionally.

2 Add the mustard seeds, cumin, paprika, garlic and ginger and stir for 1 minute. Add all the vegetables and stir to coat. Add the stock, bring to the boil, then reduce the heat and simmer, partially covered, for about 30 minutes, or until tender.

3 Place the couscous in a heatproof bowl. Add ¾ cup (185 ml/6 fl oz) of boiling water and leave to stand for 2 minutes. Add the butter, then fluff up the grains with a fork, stirring through the butter. Serve with the vegetables and a little harissa.

Chop the celery and peeled carrots into evenly sized pieces.

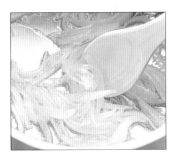

Fry onions in the oil over medium heat until soft and golden.

Add butter to the couscous and fluff up the grains using a fork.

Polenta with Spicy Vegetables

PREPARATION TIME: 30 minutes
TOTAL COOKING TIME: 1 hour 10 minutes
SERVES 4

1 tablespoon olive oil
1 large onion, sliced
4 cloves garlic, finely chopped
¼ teaspoon chilli powder
2 teaspoons ground cumin
2 teaspoons ground coriander
½ teaspoon ground turmeric
½ teaspoon ground cinnamon
2 potatoes, cubed
3 carrots, thickly sliced
1½ cups (375 ml/12 fl oz) vegetable stock
300 g (10 oz) baby yellow squash, halved
3 zucchini, cut into chunks
300 g (10 oz) pumpkin, cut into chunks
2 tablespoons chopped parsley

Polenta
1 litre vegetable stock or water
1⅓ cups (250 g/8 oz) fine polenta
100 g (3½ oz) butter, chopped
⅓ cup (35 g/1¼ oz) finely grated Parmesan

1 Heat oil in a large saucepan. Fry onion over low heat for 5 minutes, or until soft. Add garlic and spices and cook over medium heat for 3 minutes.

2 Add potato, carrot and stock. Bring to the boil, reduce heat, then cover and simmer for 10 minutes.

3 Add the squash and zucchini. Cover partially and simmer for 15 minutes. Add the pumpkin; cook for 10 minutes more, or until the vegetables are soft and the mixture is thick and gravy-like. Season well with salt and freshly cracked pepper. Remove from the heat, cover and keep warm.

4 To make the polenta, bring stock to the boil. Add the polenta in a thin stream, stirring constantly with a wooden spoon. Simmer gently for 20 minutes, stirring constantly so it doesn't stick. When thick, add the butter and Parmesan and mix until melted. Season well and serve at once.

5 Stir the parsley into the vegetables. Spoon the polenta onto serving plates, swirling it into nests with a hole in the centre. Spoon in the spicy vegetables and serve immediately.

Add the pumpkin to the partially cooked vegetable mixture.

Simmer polenta for 20 minutes, stirring constantly until thick.

When polenta has thickened, add butter and Parmesan and stir.

Mediterranean Chicken

PREPARATION TIME: 30 minutes

TOTAL COOKING TIME: 1 hour 10 minutes

SERVES 4

8 chicken thigh cutlets
2 tablespoons olive oil
150 g (5 oz) French shallots
4 cloves garlic
½ cup (125 ml/4 fl oz) white wine
425 g (14 oz) can chopped tomatoes
12 Kalamata olives
1 tablespoon red wine vinegar
2 teaspoons tomato paste
1 tablespoon oregano leaves
1 tablespoon chopped basil leaves
1 teaspoon sugar
4 slices prosciutto
1 teaspoon grated lemon rind
½ cup (30 g/1 oz) chopped parsley
1 tablespoon capers, rinsed

1 Preheat the oven to moderate 180°C (350°C/Gas 4). Remove skin and fat from the chicken thighs. Heat half the oil in a large pan and brown the chicken over high heat for 3–4 minutes on each side, then arrange in a large flameproof casserole dish.

2 Heat the remaining oil in the same pan. Add the shallots and garlic and cook over medium heat for 4 minutes, or until soft but not brown. Add the wine and bring to the boil.

3 Add the tomatoes, olives, vinegar, tomato paste, herbs and sugar. Season with salt and cracked black pepper. Boil, stirring, for 2 minutes, then pour over the chicken and cover with a tight-fitting lid. Bake for 45 minutes, or until the chicken is tender.

4 Meanwhile, place the prosciutto slices in a single layer in a frying pan, without any oil. Dry fry for 3 minutes, or until crispy, turning once. Break into large chunks and set aside.

5 Arrange the chicken on a serving dish; cover and keep warm. Transfer the casserole to the stove top and boil the pan juices for 5 minutes, or until thickened, stirring occasionally. Spoon the juices over the chicken, sprinkle with lemon rind, parsley and capers and top with the prosciutto to serve.

When the shallots and garlic are soft, add the wine.

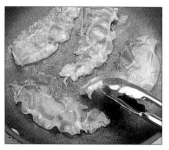

Fry prosciutto slices in a single layer in a dry frying pan.

Chicken Chasseur

PREPARATION TIME: 20 minutes
TOTAL COOKING TIME: 1 hour 30 minutes
SERVES 4

1 kg (2 lb) chicken thigh fillets
2 tablespoons oil
1 clove garlic, crushed
1 large onion, sliced
100 g (3¼ oz) button mushrooms, sliced
1 teaspoon thyme leaves
400 g (13 oz) can chopped tomatoes
¼ cup (60 ml/2 fl oz) chicken stock
¼ cup (60 ml/2 fl oz) white wine
1 tablespoon tomato paste

1 Preheat the oven to moderate 180°C (350°F/Gas 4). Trim the chicken of excess fat and sinew. Heat the oil in a heavy-based frying pan and brown the chicken in batches over medium heat. Drain on paper towels, then transfer to a casserole dish.

2 Add the garlic, onion and mushrooms to the pan and cook over medium heat for 5 minutes, or until soft. Add to the chicken with the thyme and tomatoes.

3 Combine the stock, wine and tomato paste and pour over the chicken. Cover and bake for 1¼ hours, or until the chicken is tender.

Brown chicken in hot oil and drain on paper towels.

Add garlic, onion and mushrooms to the pan and cook until soft.

Pour stock, wine and tomato paste over chicken mixture.

Gingered Duck Curry

PREPARATION TIME: 30 minutes +
30 minutes refrigeration + soaking
TOTAL COOKING TIME: 1 hour 30 minutes
SERVES 4

1.8 kg (3 lb 10 oz) duck
1 clove garlic, crushed
1 teaspoon grated fresh ginger
1 tablespoon dark soy sauce
½ teaspoon sesame oil
8 dried Chinese mushrooms
5 cm (2 inch) piece fresh ginger, peeled and
  thinly sliced
2 tablespoons yellow curry paste
2 tablespoons chopped lemon grass, white
  part only
400 ml (13 fl oz) can coconut milk
4 Kaffir lime leaves, shredded
100 g (3½ oz) Thai pea eggplants
2 teaspoons soft brown sugar
2 teaspoons fish sauce
1 tablespoon lime juice

1 Cut the duck in half by cutting down both sides of the backbone, through the breastbone. Discard the backbone. Cut each duck half into 4 portions, removing any fat. Rub the duck with combined garlic, ginger, soy sauce and oil. Refrigerate for 30 minutes.

2 Soak the mushrooms in boiling water for 20 minutes. Drain, remove the stalks and cut in half.

3 Heat a lightly oiled pan. Brown the duck over medium heat. Leaving only 1 tablespoon of fat in the pan, stir-fry the ginger, curry paste and lemon grass for 3 minutes. Stir in the coconut milk, lime leaves and ½ cup (125 ml/4 fl oz) water. Add the duck; cover and simmer gently for 45 minutes. Skim well.

4 Remove the eggplant stems; add the eggplants to the pan with the sugar, fish sauce and mushrooms. Simmer, partly covered, for 30 minutes, or until tender. Stir in lime juice to taste.

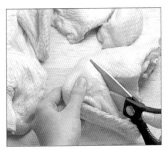

Cut duck down the middle and then cut legs and breasts in half.

Stir coconut milk, water and lime leaves into the stir-fried spices.

Remove stems from pea eggplants and add the eggplants to pan.

Spicy Venison and Vegetable Hotpot

PREPARATION TIME: 45 minutes
TOTAL COOKING TIME: 2 hours
SERVES 6

1 tablespoon olive oil
25 g (¾ oz) butter
100 g (3½ oz) pancetta, chopped
1 kg (2 lb) trimmed shoulder of venison, cut into 4 cm (1½ inch) cubes
2 onions, each cut into 8 wedges
2 cloves garlic, crushed
1 tablespoon chopped fresh ginger
1 teaspoon ground cinnamon
½ teaspoon allspice
1 teaspoon dried thyme
1 bay leaf
500 g (1 lb) tomatoes, peeled, seeded and diced
1 cup (250 ml/8 fl oz) beef stock
⅓ cup (80 ml/2¾ fl oz) orange juice
⅓ cup (80 ml/2¾ fl oz) port
200 g (6½ oz) turnip
200 g (6½ oz) parsnip

200 g (6½ oz) carrot
chopped chives, to garnish

1 Heat the oil and butter in a large, heavy-based pan. Cook the pancetta over medium heat until lightly golden. Remove and set aside.

2 Brown the venison in batches and set aside. Cook the onion until golden; add the garlic and ginger and cook for 1 minute. Add the pancetta and venison and all ingredients except the root vegetables. Bring to the boil, then reduce the heat, cover tightly and very gently simmer for 1 hour.

3 Peel the turnip, parsnip and carrot, cut into even-sized wedges and add to the pan. Cover and cook for 40 minutes, or until tender, then uncover to reduce the sauce. Season to taste, scatter with the chives and serve.

Brown the venison in batches in the hot oil and butter.

Add pancetta and venison to other ingredients except root vegetables.

Peel and cut turnip, parsnip and carrot into wedges.

Chicken Cacciatore

PREPARATION TIME: 20 minutes
TOTAL COOKING TIME: 1 hour 15 minutes
SERVES 4

1.25 kg (2 lb 8 oz) chicken pieces
2 tablespoons plain flour
1 tablespoon olive oil
1 large onion, finely chopped
2 cloves garlic, chopped
2 x 425 g (14 oz) cans tomatoes, roughly
  chopped
2 cups (500 ml/16 fl oz) chicken stock
½ cup (125 ml/4 fl oz) white wine
2 tablespoons tomato paste
1 teaspoon caster sugar
2 tablespoons chopped basil
2 tablespoons chopped parsley
½ cup (90 g/3 oz) black olives

1 Toss the chicken in the flour to coat. Heat the oil in a large, heavy-based pan and brown the chicken in batches over medium heat. Remove from the pan and drain on paper towels.

2 Cook onion and garlic in the pan for 10 minutes over low heat, stirring. Add the tomatoes, stock and wine. Bring to the boil, reduce the heat and simmer for 15 minutes. Add the tomato paste, sugar and chicken; mix well.

3 Cover and simmer for 30 minutes, then add the herbs and olives and season to taste. Simmer for another 15 minutes, stirring occasionally.

Brown chicken in batches in hot oil and drain on paper towels.

Add tomatoes, stock and wine to onion and garlic mixture.

Stir in the herbs, olives and salt and pepper to taste.

Braised Chicken with Chickpeas

PREPARATION TIME: 35 minutes
TOTAL COOKING TIME: 1 hour 35 minutes
SERVES 4

50 g (1¾ oz) butter
1 onion, roughly chopped
3 cloves garlic, crushed
1 carrot, finely chopped
½ stick celery, finely chopped
1.5 kg (2 lb) chicken pieces (about 8 portions)
⅓ cup (80 ml/2¾ fl oz) Marsala
1 cup (250 ml/8 fl oz) chicken stock
2 tablespoons lemon juice
½ cup (40 g/1¼ oz) fresh breadcrumbs
300 g (10 oz) can chickpeas, rinsed and
   drained
200 g (6½ oz) button mushrooms, sliced
2 tablespoons shredded mint
2 tablespoons chopped parsley

1 Heat half the butter in a large, heavy- based pan and cook the onion over medium heat until soft and golden. Add the garlic, carrot and celery and cook over gentle heat for 5 minutes. Remove from the pan and set aside.

2 Melt the remaining butter in the pan and brown the chicken in batches over high heat. Return all the chicken to the pan with the carrot and celery mixture. Quickly add the Marsala and stir well, scraping the sides and base of the pan. Add the stock and lemon juice, bring to the boil, then reduce the heat and simmer gently for 1 hour, stirring occasionally.

3 Remove the chicken; keep warm. In a food processor, purée the contents of the pan, then add the breadcrumbs and blend for another 15 seconds.

4 Return the chicken to the pan, pour in the purée, add the chickpeas and mushrooms and simmer, covered, for 15 minutes. Season to taste, and scatter with mint and parsley to serve.

Gently fry the garlic, carrot and celery in the butter for 5 minutes.

Pour Marsala over the vegetables and chicken, stirring well.

Add breadcrumbs to puréed pan mixture and process until smooth.

Rabbit, Chorizo and Olive Casserole

PREPARATION TIME: 35 minutes
TOTAL COOKING TIME: 2 hours 30 minutes
SERVES 4–6

150 g (5 oz) French shallots
2 tablespoons olive oil
2 kg (4 lb) rabbit pieces
2 chorizo sausages, sliced
12 pickling onions
2 cloves garlic, crushed
1 teaspoon dried thyme
1 teaspoon paprika
1 tablespoon plain flour
½ cup (125 ml/4 fl oz) white wine
1½ cups (375 ml/12 fl oz) chicken stock
1 tablespoon tomato paste
½ teaspoon grated orange rind
⅓ cup (80 ml/2¾ fl oz) orange juice
12 Kalamata olives
2 tablespoons chopped parsley
2 tablespoons chopped chives

1 Soak the shallots in boiling water for 30 seconds; drain and peel. Preheat the oven to moderate 180°C (350°F/Gas 4).

2 In a large, heavy-based pan, heat half the oil and brown the rabbit in batches over high heat, then transfer to a large casserole dish. Heat the remaining oil; fry the chorizo, shallots and onions over medium heat until soft and golden.

3 Add the garlic, thyme and paprika and cook for 1 minute. Add the flour and cook for 30 seconds.

4 Remove from the heat, pour in the wine and stir well, scraping up any bits in the pan. Return to the heat, add the stock and stir until bubbling. Add the tomato paste, rind and orange juice, then add to the rabbit and mix well. Cover and cook for 2–2¼ hours, or until the rabbit is tender. Season to taste, stir in the olives and parsley and scatter with chives to serve.

Cover shallots with boiling water, then drain and peel.

Brown the rabbit in batches in a large pan over high heat.

Heat remaining oil in pan and add chorizo, shallots and onions.

Chicken Calvados with Glazed Apples

PREPARATION TIME: 15 minutes
TOTAL COOKING TIME: 1 hour 10 minutes
SERVES 4

1.25 kg (2 lb 8 oz) chicken pieces
plain flour, seasoned with salt and freshly
    ground pepper
2 tablespoons light olive oil
30 g (1 oz) butter
1 large onion, roughly chopped
1 tablespoon chopped marjoram
1 chicken stock cube, crumbled
¾ cup (185 ml/6 fl oz) apple juice
⅓ cup (80 ml/2¾ fl oz) Calvados
¾ cup (185 ml/6 fl oz) cream

Glazed apples
2 red apples
40 g (1¼ oz) butter
2 teaspoons sugar

1 Preheat the oven to moderate 180°C (350°F/Gas 4). Trim the chicken of excess fat and sinew, then toss in the flour to coat, shaking off any excess. In a large, heavy-based pan, heat the oil and butter and brown the chicken all over, in batches if necessary. Transfer to a large casserole dish.

2 Add the onion to the pan and cook over low heat until soft but not brown. Add the marjoram, stock cube, apple juice and Calvados and bring to the boil, stirring. Season well and simmer for 5 minutes.

3 Pour the sauce over the chicken and bake, covered, for 45 minutes or until the chicken is tender. Stir in the cream and bake for 5 minutes—the sauce will be thin but delicious.

4 Meanwhile, core (but do not peel) the apples, then cut into wedges. Melt the butter in a pan, add the apples and sugar and cook over very low heat, turning occasionally, until tender and glazed. Serve with the casserole.

Toss trimmed chicken in flour to coat, shaking off any excess.

Add marjoram, stock cube, apple juice and Calvados to fried onions.

Glaze apple wedges in sugar and butter and cook until tender.

Coq au Vin

PREPARATION TIME: 20 minutes
TOTAL COOKING TIME: 1 hour
SERVES 6

2 sprigs of thyme
4 sprigs of parsley
2 bay leaves
2 kg (4 lb) chicken pieces
plain flour, seasoned with salt and freshly
  ground pepper
¼ cup (60 ml/2 fl oz) oil
4 thick bacon rashers, sliced
12 pickling onions
2 cloves garlic, crushed
2 tablespoons brandy
1½ cups (375 ml/12 fl oz) red wine
1½ cups (375 ml/12 fl oz) chicken stock
¼ cup (60 g/2 oz) tomato paste
250 g (8 oz) button mushrooms
fresh herbs, for sprinkling

1 To make the bouquet garni, wrap the thyme, parsley and bay leaves in a small square of muslin and tie well with string, or tie them between two 5 cm (2 inch) lengths of celery.

2 Toss the chicken in flour to coat, shaking off any excess. In a heavy-based pan, heat 2 tablespoons of oil and brown the chicken in batches over medium heat. Drain on paper towels.

3 Wipe the pan clean with paper towels and heat the remaining oil. Add the bacon, onions and garlic and cook, stirring, until the onions are browned. Add the chicken, brandy, wine, stock, bouquet garni and tomato paste. Bring to the boil, reduce the heat and simmer, covered, for 30 minutes.

4 Stir in the mushrooms and simmer, uncovered, for 10 minutes, or until the chicken is tender and the sauce has thickened. Remove the bouquet garni, sprinkle with fresh herbs and serve with crusty French bread.

Wrap the thyme, parsley and bay leaves in a small square of muslin.

In batches, brown the chicken in the hot oil over medium heat.

Return chicken to pan with liquids, bouquet garni and tomato paste.

Duck with Juniper Berries

PREPARATION TIME: 35 minutes
COOKING TIME: 1 hour 50 minutes
SERVES 4

1.8 kg (3 lb 10 oz) duck
1 Granny Smith apple, peeled and thinly
  sliced
1 leek, cut into large chunks
½ small red cabbage, shredded
2 bay leaves
2 sprigs of fresh thyme
6 juniper berries, lightly crushed
¼ teaspoon whole black peppercorns
1½ cups (375 ml/12 fl oz) chicken stock
1 cup (250 ml/8 fl oz) orange juice
50 g (1¾ oz) butter, chopped
2 tablespoons soft brown sugar
⅓ cup (80 ml/2¾ fl oz) cider vinegar
1½ teaspoons cornflour
sprigs of chervil, to serve

1 Preheat the oven to moderate
180°C (350°F/Gas 4). Cut the duck
in half by cutting down both sides
of the backbone and through the

breastbone. Discard the backbone. Cut each
duck half into 4 portions, removing any fat.
Brown the duck portions in a lightly oiled, heavy-
based pan over medium heat; remove and set
aside.

2 Drain the pan of all but 1 tablespoon of oil,
reserving the excess. Cook the apple until golden
all over; remove and set aside. Add I tablespoon of
the fat to the pan and lightly brown the leek.

3 Add the cabbage, bay leaves, thyme, juniper
berries and peppercorns and cook, stirring, for
10 minutes, or until the cabbage softens. Transfer
to a large flameproof casserole dish. Add the stock
and orange juice and bring to the boil. Add the
duck, pressing gently into the liquid, then cover
and bake for 1½ hours.

4 Remove the duck and keep warm. Drain the
liquid into a pan; simmer for 5 minutes, or until
reduced to 1 cup (250 ml/8 fl oz). Stir in the
butter, sugar and vinegar. Blend the cornflour with
1 tablespoon water and stir into the mixture until
it boils and thickens.

5 Stir the apple and half the
sauce into the cabbage
mixture and season to
taste. Spoon onto a serving
plate, top with the duck,
drizzle with sauce and
garnish with chervil to
serve.

*Add duck portions to cabbage,
pressing them into the liquid.*

*Stir the sugar, vinegar and butter
into the reduced sauce.*

Country Rabbit in Red Wine

PREPARATION TIME: 15 minutes
TOTAL COOKING TIME: 1 hour 30 minutes
SERVES 4

1.25 kg (2 lb 8 oz) rabbit
½ cup (125 ml/4 fl oz) olive oil
2 cloves garlic, crushed
1 sprig of rosemary, finely chopped
1 cup (250 ml/8 fl oz) red wine
½ cup (125 ml/4 fl oz) chicken stock
4 tomatoes, peeled and chopped

1 Cut the forelegs from the rabbit by cutting through the connective tissue joining the body. Cut across the back of the rabbit just above the legs, then cut the legs in half. Cut the body (saddle) of the rabbit into 2 pieces, then cut the ribcage and backbone into 4 pieces, to form 8 portions.

2 Heat the oil in a heavy-based pan. Add the rabbit, garlic and rosemary and brown the rabbit over medium heat on all sides.

3 Add the wine and stock; season with salt and freshly ground black pepper. Cover and simmer gently for 30 minutes. Add the tomatoes and cook, covered, for another 45 minutes over low heat, or until the rabbit is tender. Serve with crusty Italian bread to mop up the juices.

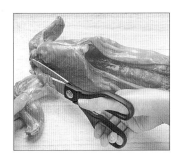
Cut the forelegs off the rabbit through connective tissue.

Cut the ribcage and body of the rabbit into 4 even pieces.

Add peeled and chopped tomatoes to pan and simmer for 45 minutes.

Moroccan Seafood with Coriander Puree

PREPARATION TIME: 50 minutes
TOTAL COOKING TIME: 50 minutes
SERVES 6

2 tablespoons olive oil
2 red onions, roughly chopped
1 red capsicum, chopped
4 cloves garlic, crushed
2 teaspoons ground cumin
1 teaspoon ground coriander
2 teaspoons sweet paprika
½ teaspoon dried chilli flakes
1 cup (250 ml/8 fl oz) chicken or fish stock
425 g (14 oz) can chopped tomatoes
4 tablespoons orange juice
1 tablespoon sugar
¼ cup (30 g/1 oz) seedless raisins
375 g (12 oz) baby new potatoes
12 raw king prawns
500 g (1 lb) baby octopus, cleaned
1 kg (2 lb) thick white fish fillets, cut into
  chunks

Coriander purée
1 cup (30 g/1 oz) fresh coriander leaves
2 tablespoons ground almonds
⅓ cup (80 ml/2¾ fl oz) extra virgin olive oil
½ teaspoon ground cumin
1 teaspoon honey

1 Heat the olive oil in a large pan and cook the onion over medium heat for about 5 minutes, or until soft. Add the capsicum and garlic and cook for another minute. Add the ground cumin, ground coriander, paprika and chilli flakes and cook until fragrant.

2 Pour in the stock, tomatoes, orange juice, sugar and raisins and bring to the boil. Add the potatoes, reduce the heat to low and gently simmer for 20–30 minutes, or until the potatoes are just tender. Season to taste.

3 Peel and devein the prawns, leaving the tails intact. Use a small sharp knife to remove the octopus heads; slit the heads open and remove the gut. Grasp the body firmly and push the beak out with your index finger; remove and discard. Add the prawns, octopus and fish to the pan and cook, covered, for 10 minutes, or until the fish flakes when tested with a fork.

4 To make the coriander purée, place the coriander leaves and ground almonds in a food processor. With the motor running, drizzle in the oil and process until smooth, then add the cumin, honey and salt to taste. Process until well combined.

5 To serve, dish the stew onto serving plates and drizzle a spoonful of purée on top. Serve with couscous and a green leaf salad.

Cioppino

PREPARATION TIME: 30 minutes +
30 minutes soaking
TOTAL COOKING TIME: 1 hour
SERVES 4

2 dried mushrooms
1 kg (2 lb) firm white fish fillets
375 g (12 oz) raw king prawns
1 raw lobster tail
12 mussels
¼ cup (60 ml/2 fl oz) olive oil
1 large onion, finely chopped
1 green capsicum, finely chopped
2–3 cloves garlic, crushed
425 g (14 oz) can crushed tomatoes
1 cup (250 ml/8 fl oz) white wine
1 cup (250 ml/8 fl oz) tomato juice
1 cup (250 ml/8 fl oz) fish stock
bay leaf
2 sprigs of parsley
6 basil leaves, chopped
1 tablespoon chopped parsley

1 Soak the mushrooms for 20 minutes. Cut the fish into bite-size pieces, removing any bones. Peel and devein the prawns, leaving the tails intact. Remove the meat from the lobster shell and cut into small pieces. Discard any open mussels; scrub the rest, remove the beards, then soak in cold water for 10 minutes. Drain the mushrooms, squeeze dry and chop finely.

2 Heat the oil in a heavy-based pan. Stirring, cook the onion, capsicum and garlic over medium heat for about 5 minutes, or until the onion is soft. Add the mushrooms, tomatoes, wine, tomato juice, stock, bay leaf, parsley sprigs and chopped basil. Bring to the boil, reduce the heat, then cover and simmer for 30 minutes.

3 Layer the fish and prawns in a large pan. Add the sauce mixture, then cover and leave on low heat for 10 minutes, or until the prawns are pink and the fish is cooked. Add the lobster and mussels and simmer for 2–3 minutes. Season to taste. Discard any unopened mussels, sprinkle with parsley, and serve with crusty bread.

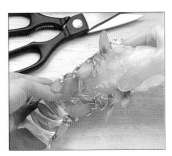

Remove lobster meat from the shell and cut into small pieces.

Add chopped mushroom, tomatoes, liquids and herbs to onion.

Add lobster and mussels when the prawns and the fish are cooked.

Seafood, Fennel and Potato Stew

PREPARATION TIME: 10 minutes
TOTAL COOKING TIME: 30 minutes
SERVES 6

1 large fennel bulb
2 tablespoons olive oil
2 leeks, thinly sliced
2 cloves garlic, crushed
½ teaspoon paprika
2 tablespoons Pernod or Ricard
200 ml (6½ fl oz) dry white wine
18 mussels, scrubbed and beards removed
¼ teaspoon saffron threads
¼ teaspoon thyme leaves
6 baby octopus
16 raw prawns, peeled and deveined
500 g (1 lb) swordfish steaks, cut into large
  chunks
400 g (13 oz) baby new potatoes
fennel greens, to garnish

1 Trim and thinly slice the fennel. Heat the oil in a large pan over medium heat. Add the fennel, leek and garlic. Stir in the paprika, season lightly and cook for 8 minutes, or until softened. Add the Pernod and wine and stir for 1 minute, or until reduced by a third.

2 Add the mussels, discarding any open ones. Cover and cook for 1 minute or until opened, discarding any which do not. Remove from the pan to cool; remove from the shells and set aside.

3 Add the saffron and thyme to the pan and cook for 1–2 minutes, stirring. Adjust the seasoning and transfer to a large, flameproof casserole dish.

4 Use a small sharp knife to remove the octopus heads. Grasp the bodies and push the beaks out with your index finger; remove and discard. Slit the heads and remove the gut. Mix the octopus, prawns, fish and potatoes into the stew. Cover and cook gently for 10 minutes, or until tender. Add the mussels, cover and heat through. Garnish with fennel greens and serve.

Trim the ends from the fennel and slice the bulb thinly.

Add the Pernod and wine to the fennel, leek and garlic mixture.

When the mussels are cool, remove them from their shells.

Lemon Grass, Coriander and Fish Stew

PREPARATION TIME: 15 minutes
TOTAL COOKING TIME: 40 minutes
SERVES 4

4 fish cutlets (200 g/6½ oz each)
plain flour, seasoned with salt and freshly
   ground pepper
2–3 tablespoons peanut oil
2 stems lemon grass
4 Kaffir lime leaves
2 onions, sliced
1 teaspoon ground cumin
1 teaspoon ground coriander
1 teaspoon finely chopped red chilli
¾ cup (180 ml/6 fl oz) chicken stock
1½ cups (375 ml/12 fl oz) coconut milk
¼ cup (15 g/½ oz) chopped coriander
2 teaspoons fish sauce

1 Preheat the oven to moderate 180°C (350°F/Gas 4). Toss the fish lightly in the flour. Heat half the oil in a large heavy-based frying pan and cook the fish over medium heat until lightly browned on both sides. Transfer to a shallow ovenproof dish.

2 Finely chop the white part of the lemon grass stems, and finely shred the lime leaves.

3 Heat the remaining oil in the pan. Add the onion and lemon grass and cook, stirring, for 5 minutes, or until the onion softens. Add the lime leaves, ground spices and chilli and stir for about 2 minutes, or until fragrant.

4 Add the stock and coconut milk and bring to the boil. Pour over the fish, then cover and bake for 30 minutes, or until the fish is tender.

5 Transfer the fish to a serving plate. Stir the chopped coriander and the fish sauce into the remaining sauce, and season to taste with salt and freshly ground pepper. Pour the sauce over the fish to serve.

Heat half peanut oil and brown floured fish over medium heat.

Finely chop the white part of lemon grass stems; shred lime leaves.

Add lime leaves, ground spices and chilli to the fried onions.

Seafood Stew with Feta and Olives

PREPARATION TIME: 20 minutes
TOTAL COOKING TIME: 35 minutes
SERVES 4

500 g (1 lb) fresh mussels
12 raw king prawns
750 g (1½ lb) firm white fish fillets
2 tablespoons olive oil
1 large onion, sliced
2 x 400 g (13 oz) cans tomatoes, chopped
2 strips lemon rind
1 tablespoon chopped lemon thyme
⅓ cup (80 ml/2¾ fl oz) dry vermouth or white wine
1 teaspoon sugar
12 black olives
125 g (4 oz) feta cheese, cubed

1 Discard any open mussels; scrub the rest and remove the beards. Place the mussels in a pan of simmering water: as soon as the shells open, place the mussels in a bowl of cold water, discarding any unopened ones. Open them up and leave on their half shells, discarding the other half.

2 Peel and devein the prawns, leaving the tails intact. Cut the fish into bite-sized pieces, removing any bones. Cover and refrigerate. Preheat the oven to moderate 180°C (350°F/Gas 4).

3 Heat the oil in a large, heavy-based pan and cook the onion over low heat for 5 minutes, or until soft but not brown. Add the tomatoes, lemon rind, lemon thyme, vermouth and sugar. Bring to the boil and season to taste. Reduce the heat, cover and simmer for 10 minutes.

4 Place the seafood in a shallow, ovenproof dish and cover with the hot sauce. Bake, covered, for 10 minutes. Add the remaining ingredients, covering the seafood with the sauce. Bake for 10 minutes, or until heated through. Serve immediately.

Scrub mussels, remove beards, and place in pan of simmering water.

Peel and devein the prawns and cut the fish into bite-sized pieces.

Add tomatoes, lemon rind, thyme, vermouth and sugar to the onion.

All our recipes are thoroughly tested in a specially developed test kitchen. Standard metric measuring cups and spoons are used in the development of our recipes. All cup and spoon measurements are level. We have used 60 g (2¼ oz/Grade 3) eggs in all recipes. Sizes of cans vary from manufacturer to manufacturer and between countries – use the can size closest to the one suggested in the recipe.

CONVERSION GUIDE

1 cup = 250 ml (9 fl oz)

1 teaspoon = 5 ml

1 Australian tablespoon = 20 ml (4 teaspoons)

1 UK/US tablespoon = 15 ml (3 teaspoons)

Where temperature ranges are indicated, the lower figure applies to gas ovens, the higher to electric ovens. This allows for the fact that the flame in gas ovens generates a drier heat, which effectively cooks food faster than the moister heat of an electric oven, even if the temperature setting is the same.

DRY MEASURES	LIQUID MEASURES	LINEAR MEASURES
30 g = 1 oz	30 ml = 1 fl oz	6 mm = ¼ inch
250 g = 9 oz	125 ml = 4 fl oz	1 cm = ½ inch
500 g = 1 lb 2 oz	250 ml = 9 fl oz	2.5 cm = 1 inch

	°C	°F	GAS MARK
Very slow	120	250	½
Slow	150	300	2
Mod slow	160	325	3
Moderate	180	350	4
Mod hot	190(g)–210(e)	375–425	5
Hot	200(g)–240(e)	400–475	6
Very hot	230(g)–260(e)	450–525	8

CUP CONVERSIONS – DRY INGREDIENTS

1 cup almonds, slivered whole = 125 g (4½ oz)

1 cup cheese, lightly packed processed cheddar = 155 g (5½ oz)

1 cup wheat flour = 125 g (4½ oz)

1 cup wholemeal flour = 140 g (5 oz)

1 cup minced (ground) meat = 250 g (9 oz)

1 cup pasta shapes = 125 g (4½ oz)

1 cup raisins = 170 g (6 oz)

1 cup rice, short grain, raw = 200 g (7 oz)

1 cup sesame seeds = 160 g (6 oz)

1 cup split peas = 250 g (9 oz)

(g) = gas (e) = electric

Note: For fan-forced ovens, check your appliance manual, but as a general rule, set the oven temperature to 20°C lower than the temperature indicated in the recipe.

INTERNATIONAL GLOSSARY

capsicum	sweet bell pepper	cornflour	cornstarch
chick pea	garbanzo bean	eggplant	aubergine
chilli	chile, chili pepper	spring onion	scallion
		zucchini	courgette

First published in 2004 by Murdoch Books Pty Limited.

Erico House, 6th Floor North, 93-99 Upper Richmond Road, Putney, London, SW15 2TG, United Kingdom.

This edition published in 2006 for Index Books Ltd, Garrard Way, Kettering, NN16 8TD, United Kingdom.

ISBN 1 74045 954 7

Printed by Sing Cheong Printing Co. Ltd. PRINTED IN CHINA.